This book is for Jude, Oliver, Declan, Ember, and Sylvan —K.H.

For my family —J.K.

I would like to thank Dr. Brian Hare for his helpful comments on this manuscript.
Any mistakes that have crept in are my own.
—Kersten Hamilton

Farrar Straus Giroux Books for Young Readers
An imprint of Macmillan Publishing Group, LLC
120 Broadway, New York, NY 10271

Color separations Embassy Graphics
Printed in China by Toppan Leefung Printing Ltd., Dongguan City, Guangdong Province
Designed by Mercedes Padró
First edition, 2021
ISBN 978-0-374-31343-2
1 3 5 7 9 10 8 6 4 2

mackids.com

Library of Congress Cataloging-in-Publication Data is available.

Our books may be purchased in bulk for promotional, educational, or business use. Please contact your local bookseller or the Macmillan
Corporate and Premium Sales Department at (800) 221-7945 ext. 5442 or by email at MacmillanSpecialMarkets@macmillan.com.

FIRST FRiEND

How Dogs Evolved from Wolves to Become Our Best Friends

Written by

Kersten Hamilton

Illustrated by

Jaime Kim

Farrar Straus Giroux
New York

Long, long ago when
nomads who hunted
through Europe and Asia
fought lean, hungry wolves
for their prey,

on a wide, wide plain where whirlwinds blew
and the grass was new,
a girl met a pup.

They jumped
and chased
and they were both very brave.

The wolf pup grew.
The girl did, too.

But everyone knew
wolves and girls could not be friends.

Still, the wolf watched as the girl hunted,
and learned.
The girl watched as the wolf hunted,
and learned.

The sun went down, the world turned round,
and years and *years* went by.

And then . . .

One day, long, long ago . . .

when people's homes were huts
of branches and hides
and wild wolves crept close
to snatch bones . . .

On a morning when winter was melting at last,
and the river was tumbling spring-flow fast,
a wolf pup met a boy
whose fingers tied knots,

scritched itches,

and sometimes shared treats.

But the wolf pup grew.
The boy did, too.
Everyone knew
the wolf and boy were not quite friends.

But the boy watched as the
wolf fished,
and laughed.
And the wolf waited as the
boy fished,
and hoped.

The sun went down,
the world turned round,
and years and *years* went by.

And then . . .

One day, long, long ago . . .

when traders brought shells to barter
for dried river fish
and Mama Wolf dug her den near
but not *too* near . . .

On a certain night
in the blue twilight,
a girl met a wolf pup

who had feathers.
The girl had dried deer meat
and knew how to trade.

The pup grew.
The girl did, too.
Everyone knew they hunted together . . .
almost like friends.

The sun went down, the world turned round,
and years and *years* went by.

And then . . .

One day, long, long ago . . .

when the valley was changing
and the people and wolves
all knew they would soon
have to find new homes far away,

while the sun burned high
and the grass grew dry,
a wolf pup met a boy
digging in a dry riverbed.
They dug down until

the hole filled up.

The wolf pup grew
and the boy did, too.
And everyone knew
they were best friends.

The wolf watched the boy leaving
and whined.
The boy looked back
and called . . .
and Dog
left the wolf pack
to follow his boy away.

The sun went down, the world turned round.
Thousands and thousands
and *thousands of years* went by.

And then . . .

Just yesterday . . .

a pup met a girl.

How Wolves Became Dogs

Humans and gray wolves lived in the same parts of the world for tens of thousands of years—they were not friends. In fact, they competed for the same **prey**.

Then, sometime between eighteen thousand and thirty-two thousand years ago, something surprising happened. Some gray wolves, perhaps in the Middle East or even East Asia, started to change. They became humans' hunting partners, then helpers, and (finally) best friends. They became dogs!

A dog is genetically 99.96 percent gray wolf, but adult dogs and adult wolves look and behave very differently.

Before dogs and wolves are eight weeks old, their behavior is very similar. Both are curious and friendly, and interested in what humans are doing. They both bark and whine for their parents' attention. After eight weeks, even wolf pups who have been raised by humans start to change. They are less interested in people than dog puppies and want to spend time with other wolves instead. Adult wolves rarely bark or whine, but adult dogs do. In fact, adult dogs act very much like wolves who never grew up! How did this happen?

The Farm-Fox Experiment

A scientist named Dmitry K. Belyaev, who studied foxes, has given us some clues. Belyaev wanted to domesticate foxes. Like wolves and dogs, very young foxes are not afraid of people. Belyaev bred foxes. Each generation, he chose the fox kits that were least afraid of humans to breed. Within eight to ten fox generations, the kits were less fox-like and more friendly. Their brains were changing. As the foxes' brains **evolved**, their bodies changed, too. Like newborn wolves, fox kits have floppy ears that stand up when they get older, wide heads that grow narrower, and short muzzles that get longer. But some of the friendly foxes' ears stayed floppy. Their heads stayed wide, and their muzzles remained shorter. Belyaev's new breed of friendly foxes looked and acted like foxes who never grew up!

Survival of the Friendliest

As hunter-gatherers started to settle into villages, some wolves found good things to eat near the humans. They liked the scraps and bones that humans threw out. They watched the humans and learned about human behavior. The least fearful and most curious wolves would have had an advantage in finding good food in trash piles. Over many generations, the least fearful wolves' brains changed. Their bodies changed as well.

The new dog-like wolves barked when danger was near. They hunted with humans. And when it was very cold, the humans and dog-like wolves may have snuggled to keep one another warm.

Being friendly helped both humans and dog-like wolves survive.

Fur Babies

Both humans and wolves are **social animals**. They live in groups that **cooperate**, and they **communicate** about how to find food and avoid danger. This made it easier for dogs and humans to learn to communicate with one another.

Some scientists who study what makes human brains special say that social communication skills are what set humans apart from other animals.

Nine-month-old babies can sometimes look where you point or follow your gaze to see what you are looking at. Dogs are the only animals that will understand without training what you are trying to communicate when you point your finger. In fact, dogs respond to eye contact and verbal and nonverbal cues from humans the way a human two-year-old would.

Of course, human babies become much, much better at communication as they grow up. But dogs' ability to communicate like human babies is part of what makes dogs and humans such good friends.

A Note About This Book

Scientists believe dogs first started living with humans somewhere in Europe or Asia. The author and illustrator imagined what the story of man's first friend would look like if it had taken place in Mongolia. They researched what life would have been like during the time wolves were evolving into dogs. No one knows what the clothing people wore looked like that long ago. But we do know that people of Asia were great innovators. At first their clothing was probably made of animal skin and sewn together using bone needles. Later, we know they learned to make textiles and dyed threads in bright colors. People hunted first with stone-tipped spears, and later learned to fletch arrows with the feathers of birds so they would fly straight. They learned to tie weights into the fishing nets they knotted. We know that their clothing and houses would have changed over the years as the climate changed. And we know that eventually, wolves had crept close to villages and evolved into dogs and followed them wherever they moved.

Selected Bibliography

Grandin, Temple, and Catherine Johnson. *Animals in Translation: Using the Mysteries of Autism to Decode Animal Behavior.* Simon & Schuster, 2005.

Hare, Brian, and Vanessa Woods. *The Genius of Dogs: How Dogs Are Smarter Than You Think.* Dutton, 2013.

Miklósi, Ádám. *Dog Behaviour, Evolution, and Cognition*, 2nd Edition. Oxford University Press, 2015.

Morey, Darcy F. "The Early Evolution of the Domestic Dog." *American Scientist*, vol. 82, no. 4, 1994, pp. 336–47. http://www.jstor.org/stable/29775234.

Trut, Lyudmila N. "Early Canid Domestication: The Farm-Fox Experiment: Foxes Bred for Tamability in a 40-year Experiment Exhibit Remarkable Transformations That Suggest an Interplay between Behavioral Genetics and Development." *American Scientist*, vol. 87, no. 2, 1999, pp. 160–69. http://www.jstor.org/stable/27857815.